Love Blooms Here

PAINTINGS BY
Glynda Turley

HARVEST HOUSE PUBLISHERS
EUGENE, OREGON 97402

Love Blooms Here

Copyright ©1997 Glynda Turley

ISBN 1-56507-711-3

All works of art reproduced in this book are copyrighted by Glynda Turley and may not be reproduced without the artist's permission. For information regarding art prints featured in this book, please contact:

> **Glynda Turley**
> P.O. Box 112
> 74 Cleburne Park Road
> Heber Springs, AR 72543
> 1-800-633-7931

Design and production by Garborg Design Works, Minneapolis, Minnesota

Harvest House Publishers has made every effort to trace the ownership of all copyrighted poems and/or quotes and obtain permission for their use. In the event of any question arising from the use of a poem or quote, we regret any error made and will be pleased to make the necessary correction in future editions of this book.

Scripture quotations are from: The Living Bible, Copyright © 1971 owned by assignment by Illinois Regional Bank N.A. (as trustee); used by permission of Tyndale House Publishers, Inc., Wheaton, Illinois; all rights reserved; The Holy Bible, New International Version®; copyright © 1973, 1978, 1984 by the International Bible Society; used by permission of Zondervan Publishing House; and the King James Version.

All rights reserved. No portion of this book may be reproduced in any form without the written permission of the Publisher.

Manufactured in China

97 98 99 00 01 02 03 04 05 06 / IM / 10 9 8 7 6 5 4 3 2 1

Love's gentle touch puts a little more *blue* in the sky, a little more *music* in the rain fall, a little more *fragrance* in the rose. When you're in *love*, the whole world looks, *sounds*, smells, and *tastes* delicious.

Walk in a place where the flowers grow sweeter and life is just a little more beautiful because love blooms here.

*I believe that love produces
a certain flowering of the
whole personality which
nothing else can achieve.*

IVAN TURGENEV

The sweetest flower that blows,
I give you as we part.
For you it is a rose,
For me it is my heart.

FREDERICK
PETERSON

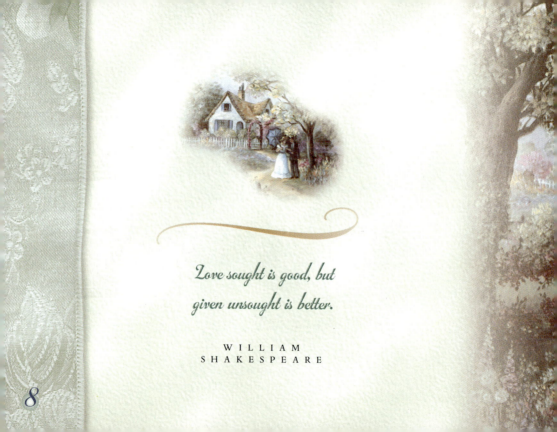

*Love sought is good, but
given unsought is better.*

WILLIAM
SHAKESPEARE

O, my luve is like a red, *red* rose,

That's newly sprung in June.

O, my *luve* is like the melodie,

That's sweetly played in tune.

As fair art *thou*, my bonie lass,

So deep in luve am I,

And I will luve thee *still*, my dear,

Till a' the seas gang dry.

ROBERT BURNS

"Can you make a little place in your heart for old Fritz?" he added, all in one breath.

"Oh, yes!" said Jo; and he was quite satisfied, for she folded both hands over his arm, and looked up at him with an expression that plainly showed how happy she would be to walk through life beside him...

They were enjoying the happy hour that seldom comes but once in any life,

the magical moment which bestows youth on the old, beauty on the plain, wealth on the poor, and gives human hearts a foretaste of heaven. The Professor looked as if he had conquered a kingdom, and the world had nothing more to offer him in the way of bliss; while Jo trudged beside him, feeling as if her place had always been there, and wondering how she ever could have chosen any other lot.

LOUISA MAY ALCOTT
Little Women

I never wrote anything worth mentioning till I was in love.

LORD BYRON

What comes from the heart, goes to the heart.

SAMUEL TAYLOR COLERIDGE

*I court others in verse:
but I love thee in prose:
And they have
my whimsies, but thou
hast my heart.*

MATTHEW PRIOR

Your brother and my sister no sooner met,

but they looked; no sooner looked but they loved;

no sooner loved but they sighed; no sooner sighed

but they asked one another the reason;

no sooner knew the reason but they

sought the remedy: and in those degrees

have they made a pair of stairs to marriage...

WILLIAM SHAKESPEARE
As You Like It

If you love someone you will be loyal

to him no matter what the cost.

You will always believe in him,

always expect the best of him,

and always stand your ground

defending him.... Love goes on forever.

1 CORINTHIANS 13

It is at the edge of the petal that love waits.

WILLIAM CARLOS WILLIAMS

*His mouth is most **sweet**: yea, he is altogether lovely.*

*This is my **beloved**; and this is my friend.*

*My beloved is gone down into his **garden**, to the beds of*

***spices**, to feed in the gardens, and to gather lilies.*

*I am my beloved's, and my **beloved** is mine.*

THE SONG OF
SOLOMON

Mr. Elton was called on, within a month from the marriage of Mr. and Mrs. Robert Martin, to join the hands of Mr. Knightley and Miss Woodhouse. The wedding was very much like other weddings, where the parties have no taste for finery or parade; and Mrs. Elton, from the particulars detailed by her husband, thought it all extremely shabby, and very inferior to her own. "Very

little white satin, very few lace veils; a most pitiful business! Selina would stare when she heard of it." But, in spite of these deficiencies, the wishes, the hopes, the confidence, the predictions of the small band of true friends who witnessed the ceremony were fully answered in the perfect happiness of the union.

JANE AUSTEN
Emma

She gave me eyes,
she gave me ears;
And humble cares,
and delicate fears;
A heart, the fountain
of sweet tears;
And love and thought
and joy.

WILLIAM
WORDSWORTH

You have stolen my heart with one glance of your eyes.

THE SONG OF SOLOMON

May the Lord make your love increase and overflow for each other...

THE BOOK OF
THESSALONIAN